Original title:
Autumn's Soft Serenade

Copyright © 2024 Creative Arts Management OÜ
All rights reserved.

Author: Tim Wood
ISBN HARDBACK: 978-9916-85-776-2
ISBN PAPERBACK: 978-9916-85-777-9

Fields of Gold

In the warmth of the setting sun,
Golden grains dance, one by one.
Whispers of winds caress each ear,
Fields of gold, a sight so dear.

Skies ablaze with hues divine,
Every stalk a treasure, a sign.
Nature's bounty in soft embrace,
Heaven's blessings on this place.

Whispering Goodbye

As twilight drapes its velvet cloak,
Silent shadows, gently spoke.
A farewell carried on the breeze,
Whispering secrets among the trees.

With heavy hearts, we hold the night,
Embracing moments, taking flight.
Though time may steal what we hold tight,
In memories' glow, we find our light.

The Season of Leafy Adieu

Crisp air heralds the autumnal grace,
Leafy wonders in a vibrant race.
Golds and reds in a swirling dance,
Nature's canvas, a fleeting chance.

Each crunch beneath our wandering feet,
Echoes of summer, bittersweet.
As branches bare in the cooler winds,
We bid farewell, where the cycle begins.

Cozy Nights Beneath Star-Laden Canopies

Beneath the quilt of twinkling stars,
Night whispers secrets of Jupiter and Mars.
Wrapped in warmth, in stories old,
We treasure moments, worth more than gold.

The flicker of flames, a crackling song,
Inviting memories where we belong.
Under the vast, celestial dome,
In cozy nights, we find our home.

Harvest Riches in the Evening Glow

Golden fields, a fruitful sight,
Harvest gathered as day turns to night.
Crimson sunsets crown the toil,
Fruits of labor from the rich soil.

In the glow of dusk, we share and feast,
Blessings abound, laughter increased.
Through toil and grace, our spirits flow,
In the bounty of life, love's true glow.

Beneath the Canopy of Change

Beneath the canopy of change, we grow,
Leaves whisper secrets only they can know.
Through seasons turning, life finds its pace,
In every shadow, there's a trace of grace.

Branches bend to tell the tales of time,
Roots entangled in the earth's soft rhyme.
In the rustle of leaves, we find our song,
A melody of right where we belong.

Harvest Moon's Gentle Glow

The harvest moon hangs low, a golden sphere,
Casting gentle light that chases off the fear.
Fields whisper stories of the toil and care,
While crickets serenade the night so fair.

In the glow of twilight, shadows blend and play,
Each grain a memory of summer's sway.
The air is sweet with the bounty of the earth,
A celebration wrapped in whispers of rebirth.

The Dance of Whispering Winds

The dance of whispering winds ignites the eve,
Caressing the trees, in spirals they weave.
With every gentle push, they carry the dreams,
Flowing like water through moonlit streams.

In the hush of the night, secrets intertwine,
Echoes of stories from valleys to pine.
Nature's breath in harmony sings soft and clear,
Revealing the magic that thrives far and near.

Colors in the Twilight

Colors in the twilight paint the sky anew,
A canvas splashed with every shade and hue.
As daylight wanes, the horizon ignites,
With whispers of beauty in magical sights.

The stars awaken, twinkling from afar,
Guiding lost wanderers beneath their star.
In the silence, the world takes a breath,
Embracing the stillness, where dreams find their depth.

Swaying Branches

In the breeze, the branches dance,
Whispers weave through leaves of green,
Each sway a fleeting, gentle chance,
Nature's art in sunlight's sheen.

A symphony of rustling sound,
Branches bent with graceful ease,
A tempest stirs, but safe and sound,
They cradle dreams with every breeze.

Softly Speaking

Words like petals, soft and light,
Drift upon the evening air,
A gentle touch, a quiet night,
Secrets shared without a care.

In the silence, hearts do bloom,
Each syllable a fleeting kiss,
Underneath the stars' bright loom,
A moment's bliss we shan't dismiss.

Mellow Days in a Fading Year

Golden leaves in the fading light,
Harvest moons and cooling air,
A simple glimpse of seasons' flight,
As mellow days bring soft despair.

The sun drapes low; its warmth retreats,
A canvas kissed by twilight's glow,
Each whispered breeze, a heartbeat beats,
In memories of days aglow.

Nature's Quiet Transition

As summer sighs in soft farewell,
The trees begin to shed their gold,
A tranquil hush, a beckoning swell,
Nature whispers stories untold.

The brook's laughter softens its tune,
Clouds like gossamer start to weave,
In twilight's charm, the world finds room,
In its quietude, we believe.

Crickets' Chirps and Candlelight

A symphony of crickets sings,
In the dusk, their chorus thrives,
Beneath the stars, the night brings flings,
Candlelight dances, warmth derives.

Soft shadows flicker on the wall,
With every chirp, the night ignites,
In this embrace, we feel it all,
Nature's pulse in gentle bites.

The Enchantment of a Quiet Grove

In a grove where whispers softly sway,
The sunlight dances, kissing leaves astray.
A tranquil heart finds rhythm in the breeze,
Nature's lullaby, a song that soothes with ease.

Mossy carpets cradle weary feet,
Shadows play with secrets, harmoniously sweet.
Birdsong weaves through branches high above,
Each note a poem, a testament of love.

Gentle streams weave tales of old and wise,
Mirroring the blue of open skies.
With every rustle, mysteries unfold,
In this enchanted grove, the stories are told.

Flickering Flames of a Cosy Hearth

The flames flicker, casting shadows warm,
A crackle dances, the evening swarm.
In this cocoon of amber glow delight,
We share our dreams, woven through the night.

Blankets hug and laughter fills the air,
Familiar faces, love beyond compare.
The world outside falls quiet and still,
While inside here, the warmth begins to thrill.

Sipping on cocoa, stories intertwine,
With every sip, our hearts align.
This cosy hearth, a refuge from the cold,
In its flickering flames, our stories unfold.

Gentle Tones of a Distant Storm

The sky draws deep with whispers of the skies,
Soft rumblings echo; nature's lullabies.
Thunder rolls gently, like a lover's song,
A symphony of shadows where we all belong.

Raindrops dance on rooftops, a rhythmic tune,
Each pitter-patter, a dream we may commune.
Lightning flashes, casting silver light,
Illuminating the path through the night.

With every gust, the trees sway in time,
A canvas alive with nature's prime.
These gentle tones, a heartbeat of the storm,
In the tempest's cradle, we find our norm.

Dreams Woven in Maple Shade

Beneath the branches where shadows play,
Whispers of hope drift through the day.
Maple leaves flutter, a delicate art,
Weave dreams of tomorrow in nature's heart.

The sun dappled patterns on the ground,
A sanctuary of thoughts, serene and profound.
In this sacred space, free minds convene,
Painting visions vivid, wild, and keen.

As the breeze carries secrets untold,
Our spirits rise, daring and bold.
In the maple's embrace, with souls unafraid,
Together we dream, in sweet shade portrayed.

Feathers of Frost in the Morning

Delicate whispers, the dawn softly calls,
Frost-kissed petals, each shimmering thrall.
Nature's embrace in a crystalline glow,
Awakens the world with a serene, gentle flow.

Silvery tendrils cling to the air,
Painting the landscape with a glistening glare.
Feathers of frost upon branches take flight,
A canvas of silence, a world bathed in light.

Stillness of a Winding Trail

A path unwinds beneath ancient trees,
Whispers of leaves dance with the breeze.
Steps echo softly on a canvas of earth,
Each moment a treasure, each turn gives birth.

In stillness, the heart finds its steady beat,
With shadows capering where daylight and dusk meet.
The journey unfolds, a serene, slow embrace,
A winding trail leads to a sacred place.

Cloudy Tints of a Pensive Sky

Clouds drift lazily, a soft, muted hue,
Beneath them, the world seems to pause for a view.
Whispers of thoughts in the winds gently play,
In shades of uncertainty, night blends with day.

An ocean of gray, where dreams often sail,
Carried by whims and the breath of the gale.
Each moment a canvas, a story unfurls,
In cloudy tints, the soul explores worlds.

Lonesome Crows in Gold Dust

Crows in the evening, a silhouette bold,
Soaring through twilight, their secrets unfold.
Against the gold dust of a setting sun,
They weave their dark tales, till the day is done.

Lonesome they linger, on branches they rest,
Guardians of stories, in the hush they invest.
A chorus of echoes, of life intertwined,
In the fading light, the crows gently remind.

The Symphony of Crickets' Song

In twilight's embrace, the crickets play,
A melody woven in the fading day.
Whispers of night with a rhythmic grace,
Nature's orchestra in this sacred space.

Under the stars, their serenade hums,
Echoing softly as the night succumbs.
Filling the air with stories untold,
In the symphony of crickets, life unfolds.

Majestic Trees in Majestic Gold

Beneath autumn's touch, the leaves ignite,
Gold and amber blaze in the soft twilight.
Majestic trees stand with timeless grace,
Guardians of secrets in their sheltering embrace.

Roots intertwined in earth's tender hold,
Each branch a chapter, each leaf a fold.
In silence, they witness the seasons' dance,
Majestic trees hold nature's romance.

The Quietude of Forgotten Trails

Amidst the woods where the wildflowers sigh,
Lies a path untrodden, a whispering sigh.
Forgotten trails weave stories of old,
Each step a promise in the silence bold.

Moss carpets the ground, a soft, gentle bed,
Where echoes of laughter and memories tread.
Nature keeps secrets, a soft sacred gale,
In the quietude found on forgotten trails.

Clouds that Weep with Grace

In the azure sky, soft clouds drift and bow,
With tears that fall gently, like a whispered vow.
They weep for the earth, yet their sorrow sings,
Nurturing life with the love that it brings.

Graceful reflections in puddles they leave,
A mirror of beauty, a moment to cleave.
In every drop, a story, a trace,
Of the clouds that weep with such tender grace.

Nostalgic Melodies of Dusk

As the sun dips low, a golden hue,
Whispers of stories the night will imbue.
Songs of the past in the twilight air,
Memories dance in the cool evening glare.

Crickets compose with a symphonic grace,
Echoes of laughter in this sacred space.
Each note a reminder of joys held so dear,
In the arms of the dusk, the heart draws near.

Fleeting moments like fireflies' glow,
Fading away but forever we know.
Within these soft shadows where time bends low,

Nostalgic melodies of dusk gently flow.

The Caress of Cool Breezes

In the still of the morn, a whispering sigh,
The cool breeze awakens, in freedom it flies.
Gentle embrace of the earth's tender breath,
Carries the scents of life, love, and death.

Lemonade laughter spills from the trees,
Echoing sweetness within the soft leaves.
Every flutter, a dance, in this tranquil space,
Nature's soft fingers weave dreams in the lace.

The sighs of the meadows, of flowers and streams,
Breezes harmonize with suns and moonbeams.
Through meadows and valleys, this chorus will glide,
The caress of cool breezes—our hearts open wide.

Shadows of Harvest Dreams

In fields where the sunflowers lift their proud heads,
Shadows stretch long where the harvest now spreads.
With golden grains rustling in breezy embrace,
We gather our dreams, in this bountiful place.

Wheat dances like whispers of lullabies sweet,
Echoes of labor in rhythm, in beat.
Hands stained with soil, embraces of toil,
Fruits of our work from the rich, fertile soil.

The twilight sky dons a velvet-like gown,
As night gathers round, wearing dusk's gentle crown.
In shadows of harvest our hopes brightly gleam,
Rooted in passions, we sow our bold dreams.

Echoes of a Wistful Breeze

Through the tangled branches, soft breezes play,
Carrying whispers at close of the day.
Echoes of laughter, of love lost and gained,
Dance in the twilight, both joyful and pained.

Wistful reminders of paths intertwined,
The heart's gentle longing for moments defined.
Crickets serenade under darkening skies,
While memories linger like stars in our eyes.

Promises linger, unspoken but clear,
In the sigh of the evening that draws us near.
With echoes of a breeze, in twilight's embrace,
We find in the stillness our own sacred space.

The Palette of a Setting Sun

Crimson spills across the sky,
Brush strokes of amber and gold,
Each fading light, a whispered sigh,
As day's warm tale begins to fold.

Clouds dance in hues of violet dreams,
The horizon cradles the day's sweet loss,
Nature listens as sunlight beams,
In this twilight painted gloss.

Birds take flight in a fiery glow,
Horizon kissed by evening's hand,
Each stroke a memory we cherish so,
As night unfolds its velvet strand.

In this palette, our hearts reside,
A canvas of moments, bright and brief,
The sun dips low, the shadows glide,
In the silence, we find relief.

Crisp Air and Feathered Friends

In the stillness of autumn's breath,
Crisp air weaves through dancing leaves,
A melody rings of life and death,
As nature's song, the heart believes.

Feathered friends flit, a joyous flight,
Chirps and whistles fill the air,
Beneath the sun's warm, golden light,
They gather 'round without a care.

Branches swaying with playful ease,
A chorus of wings in playful chase,
Their harmonies blend with the rustling trees,
In this moment, a sacred space.

As shadows stretch and daylight wanes,
These fleeting friends, a sight to see,
In the chill of air, their joy remains,
A testament to wild, free glee.

Harvest Chimes in the Breeze

Golden fields dance in the gentle wind,
Where crops sway with whispers of delight,
Harvest chimes where the stories begin,
Beneath the sun's embracing light.

Pumpkins plump and apples gleam,
Cornstalks rustle with secrets old,
Nature provides in a bountiful dream,
As autumn's tapestry, rich and bold.

Children laugh, their voices rise,
Gathering remnants of the year's sweet toil,
Underneath the expansive skies,
A season's joy, the earth's rich soil.

In every chime, a promise sings,
Of future blooms and rains anew,
In harvest's grace, the heart still clings,
To the gifts of nature, pure and true.

Flickers of Lanterns in the Gloom

Flickers dance where shadows meet,
Lanterns glow with a gentle grace,
Carried whispers on the breeze,
In this quiet, sacred space.

Each flicker tells a tale of night,
Stories woven in amber light,
Against the darkness, a vibrant fight,
A beacon in the quiet fright.

Gathered friends, their faces bright,
Around the glow, hearts entwine,
In these moments, we ignite,
The warmth of laughter, hearts combine.

In the gloom, hope always warms,
Flickers guiding, gentle, true,
Through the shadows, love transforms,
In lanterns' glow, we find our view.

Raindrops on Weathered Trails

Raindrops fall on paths long worn,
Whispers of the storms that have passed,
Each droplet sings of memories sworn,
On this asphalt, shadows are cast.

Puddles gather, reflecting skies,
Cloaked in hues of misted grey,
The world slows down, as nature sighs,
In tranquil pools, time slips away.

A Canvas of Dried Petals

Petals lie in sunlit decay,
A canvas rich with colors lost,
Each fragment tells of the dance of May,
And echoes of love, no matter the cost.

Gently crumbled, yet still they gleam,
Soft whispers of what once was bright,
In their stillness, dreams softly dream,
Dancing under the fading light.

The Scent of Woodsmoke and Memories

In the air, woodsmoke lingers low,
A warm embrace from the evening fire,
It conjures tales from long ago,
Of laughter shared and dreams that aspire.

Breeze carries whispers, secrets unfold,
Embers flicker like stars in the night,
Each scent a memory, a story retold,
In the heart's hearth, warmth ignites.

Flickering Shadows in the Late Sun

Beneath the gaze of the setting Sun,
Shadows stretch like lazy dreams,
As day bids farewell, adventures begun,
In the warmth of dusk, nothing's as it seems.

Chasing the light, we dance on the grass,
Flickering moments, fleeting and bright,
In twilight's embrace, we gracefully pass,
A tapestry woven of day and night.

Nature's Painted Farewell

Amber leaves descend like whispered sighs,
In the twilight glow, the horizon lies.
Breezes carry secrets, a soft, sweet song,
As the sun dips low, where shadows belong.

Crimson blushes weave through the gentle trees,
A tapestry of colors dancing in the breeze.
The day retreats, with a painter's final stroke,
In nature's embrace, the silence awoke.

Serene Reflections in Still Waters

Mirrored whispers cradle the starlit sky,
Ripples of silver where quiet dreams lie.
Moonlight spills softly on the tranquil shore,
Revealing secrets that waters implore.

Gentle caresses of night's cool breath,
Bathe the world softly, as daylight meets death.
In this sacred silence, the heart finds its way,
To the serene reflections that night holds at bay.

A Quilt of Nature's Bounty

Fields of gold stretch under the azure expanse,
A patchwork of colors invites us to dance.
Each blossom, a story embroidered with care,
In the heart of the earth, our joys laid bare.

Mountains stand guard, like ancient wise friends,
Cradling the valleys where the river bends.
Nature assembles her quilt every day,
In a symphony vibrant, where wildflowers sway.

The Ink of Evening Skies

Brushstrokes of twilight, a canvas ablaze,
With hues of deep violet, and soft-burning gaze.
Stars begin to shimmer, like ink from a pen,
Sketching the moments when day meets its end.

Clouds drift like thoughts, in a dreamlike parade,
Each whispered farewell in the dusk's cool shade.

The sky's gentle palette unveils what we see,
In the ink of the evening, our souls feel free.

The Gracious Weaving of Time

In the loom of stars where dreams entwine,
Threads of silver whisper tales divine.
Moments dance like shadows in twilight's glow,
Each heartbeat stitches the fabric we know.

Seasons pass in a gentle, flowing stream,
Echoes of laughter, fragments of a dream.
Days blend softly, like colors in the sky,
Binding our stories as years drift by.

Memories Brewed in Hearth's Glow

In the warmth of the hearth where stories are spun,
The crackling fire hums, its work never done.
Steam from the kettle rises like our past,
Memories brew slowly, a fragrant contrast.

Laughter and love linger thick in the air,
Rich as the cocoa and sweetened with care.
We gather around as dusk settles near,
In the heart of this home, we hold what is dear.

A Gentle Farewell Under Fiery Canopy

Beneath the arching boughs of an autumn embrace,
Leaves like embers drift, in a soft, swirling grace.

The sun dips low, a painter's soft sigh,
As shadows stretch long under a fiery sky.

Whispers of wind carry secrets untold,
Promises woven in hues of bright gold.
With every farewell, a new journey begins,
In the circle of life, the dance never ends.

The Walking Poem of the Season

Through fields adorned in blossoms so bright,
Each step we take is a stanza of light.
The breeze sings softly, a muse on the run,
Guiding our hearts beneath the warm sun.

With every rustle of leaves in the air,
Nature composes a melody rare.
As seasons shift, we find rhythm and rhyme,
In the walking poem that flows through all time.

Hushed Paths of Golden Silence

In the twilight's soft embrace, shadows play,
Golden leaves whisper secrets of the day.
Footsteps muted on the winding way,
Each moment lingers, sweetly on display.

Breezes carry tales of ages past,
As time stands still, horizons contrast.
Nature's hush, a spell that holds us fast,
In this golden silence, memories cast.

Warmth in the Chill of Dusk

The sun dips low, painting the skies,
A canvas of amber, where soft shadows rise.
Chill weaves through veins, but warmth within lies,
Hearts aglow, despite the night's sighs.

Firelight dances with flickering grace,
Embers crackle, each one finds its place.
In the gathering gloom, we share our embrace,
Finding solace in the dusk, a tender space.

The Dance of Dwindling Days

Leaves twirl softly, surrendered by time,
In the waning light, they form nature's rhyme.
Days slip away, like a fading chime,
A fleeting waltz, both tragic and sublime.

The sun's farewell kisses the night's veil,
Whispers of twilight tell a bittersweet tale.
In this graceful descent, none can derail,
The dance of dwindling days, we inhale.

Reflections of a Gathering Storm

Dark clouds converge, a symphony swells,
Nature's voice thunders, a tale it tells.
Raindrops gather, like secrets in shells,
Preparing to burst, as the tension compels.

The air is electric, charged with the night,
Lightning scribbles stories in brilliant white.
In the heart of the tempest, chaos takes flight,
Reflections of a storm, beautiful fright.

A Tapestry of Amber and Crimson

In autumn's glow, the leaves descend,
A dance of amber, a story to send.
Crimson whispers in the gentle breeze,
Nature's palette brings the heart at ease.

Beneath the boughs where shadows play,
Golden hues ignite the waning day.
Each branch adorned with nature's art,
A tapestry woven, a work of heart.

Gentle Echoes of Nature's Farewell

As daylight dwindles, a hush descends,
Nature's serenade, where silence lends.
The rustling leaves, a soft goodbye,
Echoes linger as the sun dips shy.

Crickets chirp in the fading light,
A symphony born of the looming night.
In twilight's arms, the world holds its breath,
Embracing the beauty in nature's death.

Twilight's Brush on Graying Skies

Colors blend as day meets night,
Twilight's brush paints the fading sight.
Soft pastels, with strokes so light,
A canvas whispered in quiet delight.

Clouds gather like shadows cast,
The moment stills, yet fades so fast.
As stars awaken in the dark,
The universe hums with a silent spark.

The Symphony of Fading Light

The sun retreats, a blazing fire,
Fading notes of a golden choir.
Shadows stretch on the cool gray earth,
As dusk unfolds its quiet mirth.

Each ray lingers, a tender sigh,
Melodies drift as the light says goodbye.
In the stillness, we find our place,
Wrapped in the warmth of twilight's embrace.

Twilight in Amber Hues

As daylight wanes in shades of gold,
The whispers of the night unfold,
Amber hues that softly blend,
A canvas where the day must end.

Stars peek through the velvet sky,
As fleeting moments gently sigh,
The world wrapped in a warm embrace,
In twilight's calm, we find our place.

Fading Warmth

The sun dips low, a fiery gleam,
As shadows stretch, the daylight streams,
A chill creeps in, the warmth departs,
Leaving echoes in restless hearts.

Candles flicker, a soft goodbye,
In the quiet, we ponder why,
Each radiance must find its fate,
In fading warmth, we contemplate.

Lingering Echoes

In the silence, echoes dwell,
Of whispered thoughts and tales to tell,
Memories drift like autumn leaves,
In the heart, the spirit weaves.

Soft reverberations in the night,
Carrying dreams on wings of light,
Each moment etched, a fleeting trace,
Lingering like a soft embrace.

Rustling Secrets Among the Trees

Beneath the boughs where shadows play,
The rustling leaves hold secrets sway,
Whispers travel on the breeze,
Tales of time, rustling secrets among the trees.

Branches sway with ancient grace,
Guardians of this sacred space,
In every rustle, a story spun,
Nature's rhythm, forever young.

A Symphony of Crisp Air

When morning breaks with sharp delight,
A symphony of crisp air takes flight,
Each breath a note, a melody,
Nature's orchestra, wild and free.

Leaves crackle beneath our stride,
An encore of the autumn tide,
In this concert, we find our share,
In harmony, the crisp, cool air.

Whispers of the Falling Leaves

In the woods where silence weaves,
The secrets carried by the breeze,
Rustling softly through the trees,
Whispers of the falling leaves.

Golden hues paint autumn's grace,
Nature's artwork, time laid bare,
A gentle touch, a warm embrace,
With every breath, the world a prayer.

Crisp air lingers, memories cling,
Of summer days and skies of blue,
As twilight sings its closing string,
And shadows dance, while light bids adieu.

In this moment's still retreat,
Each leaf a story, old yet new,
They spiral down in soft defeat,
Leaving paths for dreams to strew.

Golden Hues of Dusk

As day surrenders to twilight's call,
The sky ignites with fiery delight,
Golden hues where shadows fall,
Embracing the warmth of the fading light.

Clouds painted softly in rose and gold,
Whispers of daylight quietly fade,
A story of time, forever told,
In the tapestry of dusk, gently laid.

Crickets begin their evening song,
The world transforms with each passing breath,
In this brief moment, where we belong,
Life dances on the edge of death.

With every sigh, the stars awake,
A blanket of dreams to guide our way,
In the golden hues, memories take,
As night wraps the beauty of day.

The Harvest Moon's Lullaby

Beneath the harvest moon's soft glow,
Fields of gold await the reaping,
A tender breeze begins to flow,
Nature sings, and all is sleeping.

Grains wave gently in the night's embrace,
Stars aligned in perfect tune,
While shadows stretch and time slows its pace,
In the embrace of a sleepy afternoon.

Crickets join in a rhythmic rhyme,
As earth rejoices in the bounty shared,
Each note a promise, a glimpse of time,
In the quiet night, we lay prepared.

The moon, a guardian of dreams unfurled,
Watches o'er the land with gentle pride,
In the heart of autumn's painted world,
The harvest moon's lullaby, our guide.

Rustling Dreams in the Chilly Breeze

In the chill of a whispering night,
Dreams take flight on fragile wings,
Rustling softly between dark and light,
Each breath a tale that twilight sings.

Autumn's chill wraps hearts with ease,
As leaves perform their final dance,
Carried softly by the breeze,
Where hope and memory weave their romance.

The stars peek through their velvet shrouds,
Each a secret waiting to be known,
In the symphony of night, we're proud,
As rustling dreams beckon us home.

With every gust that sweeps the land,
A promise held in the night's embrace,
These rustling dreams, like grains of sand,
Guide our souls to a loving place.

Whispered Goodbyes to the Sun

In the silence of the gloaming light,
Shadows stretch, as day turns night,
A golden orb sinks low and sighs,
With whispered goodbyes, the sun complies.

Fingers of dusk reach for the sky,
Embracing stars as they start to fly,
While the world holds its breath in pause,
Preserving the warmth of its fleeting cause.

A Mosaic of Earth's Farewell

In patches of color, the earth lays bare,
A quilt of whispers, woven with care,
Each leaf a memory, each stone a song,
In the mosaic of earth, we find where we belong.

As autumn's brush dips in decayed gold,
Tales untold, in silence unfold,
With every step, the ground exhales,
A farewell whispered in the gentle gales.

Watercolors of a Wistful Sky

In strokes of blue and hints of grey,
The sky spills secrets of the day,
Clouds blush with the heart's tender ache,
In watercolors, dreams gently wake.

Each drop of rain a story to tell,
Of moments fleeting, in glistening shell,
As the twilight wraps the world in a sigh,
Painting the horizon, where memories lie.

The Labyrinth of Twisting Vines

In the garden's heart, where shadows entwine,
A labyrinth whispers through twisting vine,
Every turn leads to secrets anew,
Stories of old, wrapped in morning dew.

Step carefully here, where time seems to pause,
Nature's embrace reveals hidden flaws,
In the tangled paths where dreams often quiver,
The soul finds truth that makes the heart shiver.

Amber Petals on Soft Ground

In gardens where the sun does kiss,
Amber petals softly lie,
Whispers of the morning's bliss,
Carried gently on the sigh.

Beneath the boughs, in dappled shade,
Each step brings forth a fragrant trail,
Nature's brush, with colors laid,
A tapestry where dreams set sail.

Fluttering wings, a dance of light,
Bees hum sweetly as they roam,
In this realm, all feels so right,
Where heart finds peace and spirit's home.

Golden hues and verdant greens,
A symphony of life unfolds,
In every nook, a secret leans,
Tales of beauty waiting, told.

Celestial Canopy of Stars

Beneath the vast, unending dome,
Where dreams and stardust weave and play,
The universe, our cosmic home,
In silent wonder, we drift away.

Each twinkle tells a story bright,
Of ancient worlds and futures vast,
In night's embrace, our hearts take flight,
As constellations hold us fast.

A silver path, the moon shall lead,
Through galaxies that softly hum,
In this embrace, we plant a seed,
Of hopes and dreams yet to become.

So lift your eyes and find your spark,
In every heartbeat, every sigh,
For in this night, the light ignites,
A love that reaches for the sky.

Sunlight's Last Dance on the Water

As day bows down to evening's grace,
The sun spills gold upon the sea,
In rippling waves, a warm embrace,
A shimmering dance, wild and free.

Reflections twirl in fading light,
A canvas brushed by nature's hand,
With every blink, the day takes flight,
And dreams take root upon the sand.

The horizon wears a fiery crown,
While whispers of the night begin,
As twilight softly settles down,
The world exhales, the day wears thin.

In this sweet hush, we find our peace,
As stars emerge to greet the shore,
With every wave, our worries cease,
The heart sets sail, forevermore.

Moments of Quiet Reflection

In stillness found beneath the trees,
Where whispers of the world do fade,
A moment's pause, a gentle breeze,
Invites the soul to unafraid.

The river sings a tranquil tune,
As thoughts meander, soft and slow,
With every sigh, we drift to noon,
In quietude, our spirits grow.

The mind, a canvas, colors blend,
With memories brushed in hues of gold,
In silence, each heart learns to mend,
As stories of the past unfold.

So close your eyes, let worries fly,
In moments rich, hear nature's song,
For in this peace, the heart will sigh,
And here, in stillness, we belong.

Celebrating the Hard-Won Fruits

In fields where labor's songs are sung,
The fruits of toil from earth are wrung,
With every seed, a story told,
Of dreams and hopes in harvest gold.

Each drop of sweat, a blessing we reap,
In rows of bounty, our promise we keep,
Sharing joy in every bite,
In unity, we bask in the light.

The sun's warm kiss, the rain's sweet grace,
Bring life to every sacred space,
Together we stand, our spirits soar,
In gratitude, we celebrate more.

So lift your glass to the ground we tread,
To the love and care that daily is spread,
For in every fruit, our labor shines,
A testament to the heart in the vines.

Mellow Tones of Rustling Corn

As evening drapes in twilight's veil,
Rustling corn whispers a gentle tale,
Golden stands in the soft, warm breeze,
Swaying rhythm, nature's melodies.

Each stalk a guardian, wise and tall,
With secrets held, like shadows that fall,
In amber hues, the sunset glows,
Painting the world in soft repose.

Crickets play their evening song,
A symphony where we belong,
In this twilight, the heart finds peace,
As nature's spirit grants sweet release.

Beneath the stars, the cornfield sighs,
In the night's embrace, tranquility lies,
With every whisper from the rows,
Mellow tones of life gently flows.

Secrets of a Starlit Night

Beneath the vast, eternal sky,
Where dreams and wishes freely fly,
The stars unveil their ancient light,
Whispering secrets of the night.

In silent heavens, stories unfold,
Of wanderers brave and hearts of gold,
Each flicker a memory, lost and found,
In the soft glow, our hopes surround.

The moon, a sentinel, watches near,
Casting shadows, dispelling fear,
In the stillness, we find our way,
Guided by starlight, night and day.

So close your eyes, let the wonder reign,
In the cosmos, there's no pain,
For in this dance of light and dark,
We find the echo of our spark.

The Elegy of Nature's Cycle

In the heart of the woods, where silence reigns,
Nature weaves her intricate chains,
Seasons shift like a whispered sigh,
From blooming grace to the autumn's goodbye.

Each leaf that falls is a tale retold,
Of life and loss, of vibrant gold,
In winter's arms, the world lies still,
Awaiting the sun's warm, gentle thrill.

The rivers flow with memories clear,
Their currents embrace all that draws near,
In the dance of time, we come and go,
Embracing the ebb, the pulse of the flow.

So let us honor this timeless art,
The cycle of nature, the beating heart,
For every end brings a new start,
In the grand elegy, we play our part.

Whispered Promises of Renewal

In the quiet dawn where shadows play,
Whispers of life in the misty gray,
Promises woven on the threads of air,
Awakening dreams from their slumbered lair.

Buds of green push through the frost,
In every heartbeat, no moment is lost,
The earth sighs gently, a lover's embrace,
In a world reborn, we find our place.

Hope dances lightly on the zephyr's breath,
Carving new paths through the echoes of death,
Every sunset paints a canvas anew,
In whispered promises, we rise and renew.

The Melancholy of Fading Light

As the sun dips low, a golden tear,
The horizon swallows the day's last cheer,
A symphony fades in the dimming glow,
Painting the world in shades of woe.

Silhouettes linger against twilight's sigh,
Echoes of laughter in the night sky die,
The heart, once bold, now whispers in doubt,
In the tender embrace of shadows, we shout.

Memories drift like the leaves on the breeze,
Fragments of joy tangled in mournful pleas,
Yet in this sorrow, a beauty remains,
In the melancholy of light, love sustains.

Nature's Final Bow

The autumn leaves perform their last dance,
Falling slowly, caught in fate's trance,
Nature's curtain drawn with a rustling sigh,
A symphony ending as seasons comply.

Crisp air whispers tales of cycles and time,
Each withered branch a verse, each shadow a rhyme,
The earth wears her garments of amber and gold,
In this grand finale, stories unfold.

Yet within decay lies a promise of grace,
For every ending finds a new space,
As winter's embrace invites silence profound,
Nature bows gently, peace all around.

The Restlessness of Dying Days

In the twilight hours, where shadows creep,
Restlessness dances, awakening sleep,
Each ticking clock counts the moments we grasp,

As time slips through our fingers, a fleeting clasp.

The air thickens heavy with the weight of the past,
Whispers of memories, echoes that last,
Beneath the twilight's hue, we search for the light,

In the lingering shadows, we battle the night.

Hope flickers dimly as dreams start to fade,
Yet through the stillness, our hearts remain swayed,
For in every ending, there's a fire that stays,
A restless longing that never betrays.

Luminescence of Golden Moments

In the hush of twilight's glow,
   golden fringes dance and flow,
  laughter spills like molten light,
    weaving magic in the night.

Each second glimmers, bright and bold,
    a tapestry of stories told,
  within our hearts, they softly dwell,
  a symphony we weave so well.

Shadows lengthen, but we remain,
counting treasures without disdain,
for every moment holds a dream,
   reflected in a silver stream.

So let us gather, hand in hand,
savoring the sands of time's strand,
and in these golden hours, we find,
the precious warmth that binds mankind.

The Sorrows of a Withering Vine

In a garden once lush and fair,
now whispers echo in the air,
the vine that climbed with vibrant grace,
laments its slow and weary pace.

Leaves curl in longing, deep and shy,
as petals flutter, saying goodbye,
each tendril droops, a tale of loss,
beneath the weight of silent cross.

The sun that kissed the verdant skin,
now casts a shadow, deep within,
while memories of warmth ignite,
the wistful heart, alone in night.

Yet even decay holds beauty's thread,
a cycle of life where dreams are wed,
in sorrow's depths, hope might entwine,
for every end, a chance to shine.

Soft Embraces of Winding Paths

Along the trails where shadows glide,
soft whispers of the earth abide,
each step a promise, rich and rare,
as nature weaves her tender care.

The trees entwined in gentle dance,
invite the wanderer's fleeting glance,
through fog and light, they softly lead,
to hidden dreams and unspoken creed.

As rivers hum their timeless song,
the heart finds solace, where it belongs,
with every bend, a secret to unveil,
in soft embraces, love shall prevail.

So venture forth, embrace the roam,
for winding paths will guide you home,
with every turn, let spirit flow,
in nature's arms, forever glow.

Echoes in the Orchard

Beneath the boughs where fruits do sway,
echoes dance at close of day,
whispering tales of seasons past,
in every rustle, memories cast.

The apples blush, the pears stand tall,
each harvest sings a whispered call,
where laughter blooms and shadows play,
in orchards bright where children sway.

Time weaves stories, rich and deep,
of promises made and secrets to keep,
while petals fall like whispered songs,
in the gentle breeze that carries long.

So linger here, in nature's grace,
let echoes wrap you in their embrace,
for life is sweet in this sacred space,
where hearts convene and love finds place.

Beneath a Tapestry of Gold

A whisper of autumn in the air,
Leaves dance gently without a care,
Crisp sunlight filters through every tree,
A golden canvas, wild and free.

Branches bow with a heavy crown,
Nature dons her finest gown,
Every hue a tale to share,
Beneath the sky, a dreamer's lair.

Footsteps crunch on a carpet bright,
Golden glory in soft twilight,
Moments captured, fleeting, bold,
Stories woven in threads of gold.

So let us wander, hand in hand,
Through this wonder, this gilded land,
Embrace the beauty all around,
Beneath a tapestry of gold, profound.

Ember Dreams of a Cool Evening

As shadows slip into the night,
The fire whispers, flickering light,
Embers dance with a soft embrace,
Cooling breezes brush my face.

Stars awaken, one by one,
Each a story, a tale begun,
Gathered round, where laughter flows,
In ember dreams, serenity grows.

Cool night wraps the world in ease,
Rustling leaves sway with the breeze,
In this moment, all feels right,
Wrapped in warmth beneath the night.

Let the nightingale serenade,
In the glimmering twilight shade,
Ember dreams ignite the soul,
In this cool evening, I feel whole.

Lullabies Under Maple Branches

Crimson leaves like whispers fall,
Underneath the maple, I hear them call,
A lullaby woven in the breeze,
Softly spinning through the trees.

The branches cradle gentle sighs,
As twilight lingers and daylight dies,
A symphony of twilight's grace,
With every note, a warm embrace.

Time dances slow in this sacred nook,
Where dreams unfold like a storybook,
Under the canopy where shadows blend,
Lullabies sing, and worries mend.

In the hush of the evening's glow,
Emotions rise and softly flow,
Underneath the maple's reach,
Life's gentle lessons, nature's speech.

The Last Sigh of Summer's Breath

The sun drips low, a golden tear,
As summer bids its slow farewell here,
Fields turn in hues of amber and rust,
In the fading light, we place our trust.

Cicadas murmur a final song,
Calling us where the shadows belong,
The air still warm with memory's taste,
Each moment precious, too sweet to waste.

With every breeze, nostalgia sways,
Recalling long, sun-filled days,
The laughter echoes, softly heard,
In the whispers of wings, love's great word.

So let us linger, let us reflect,
On the fleeting joys we won't forget,
For in this sigh, as seasons change,
The last breath of summer feels so strange.

Glistening Dew at Daybreak

In the hush of morning's light, a treasure lies,
Soft glistening dew, where the grass complies,
Each droplet a gem, reflecting dawn's embrace,
A fleeting moment, nature's gentle grace.

The world awakens, kissed by the sun,
Birds chirp sweetly, the new day has begun.
With every breath, a promise interweaves,
In this tranquil scene, the heart believes.

Petals unfurl, adorned in crystal beads,
Whispers of night's secrets, the earth concedes.
Nature's canvas, painted fresh and bright,
A symphony of colors, pure delight.

As shadows retreat, and the light expands,
The glistening dew, like soft silken strands.
Each droplet will fade, as the sun climbs high,
Yet in memory linger, as hours drift by.

Caramel Hues on the Horizon

As daylight wanes, the sky starts to blush,
Caramel hues blend in a soft golden rush,
Brushstrokes of amber, a sweet, tender glow,
Whispers of twilight begin to bestow.

Mountains stand tall, cloaked in soft mist,
Embers of sunset, a painter's soft twist.
Every hue mingles, a harmonious tune,
Singing the promise of the rising moon.

Fields bathed in gold, where shadows now play,
The world finds its peace at the close of the day.
Birds serenade the dusk in flowing flight,
As stars awaken in the velvet night.

In this serene moment, the heart takes its rest,
Savoring sweetness, the day's quiet best.
Caramel hues fading, yet love remains,
Like echoes of laughter in gentle refrains.

The Aroma of Earth's Renewal

With the first drop of rain, the earth takes a sigh,
Releasing its secrets as clouds drift by.
The aroma of soil, rich and profound,
Affirming the cycle, life's dance all around.

Green shoots appear, peeking through the ground,

A chorus of life in soft whispers resound.
Each fragrant breath tells of seasons past,
A tapestry woven, resilient and vast.

Petals unfurl in colors that thrill,
Each bloom a story, each leaf a quill.
The scent of rebirth fills the air anew,
A promise of growth in each morning dew.

Beneath ancient trees, shadows deepen and sway,

In the nurturing arms of the earth, we play.
The aroma of life, tenderly made,
In this fragrant embrace, all worries will fade.

Murmurings in the Leaf-Laden Path

Amidst the foliage, whispers softly sway,
Murmurings of seasons, in shades of decay.
Leaves carpeting earth, a crunch with each step,
Tales of the past in the silence adept.

Sunlight dapples through branches, casting a glow,
A dance of shadows, where breezes do flow.
In the pathway of dreams, stories entwine,
Each rustling leaf echoes, a memory divine.

Squirrels but dart, chasing flickering light,
The rustle of leaves, a soft, fleeting plight.
In this wooded refuge, spirits find peace,
From the weight of the world, a gentle release.

So wander these trails, where nature's heart beats,

In murmurings soft, the world's rhythm repeats.
Through leaf-laden paths, let your soul wander free,
In the embrace of the forest, find tranquility.

Frost-kissed Mornings in the Meadow

In the quiet dawn, where silence reigns,
Frost-kissed petals shimmer like diamonds.
The soft breath of winter, a gentle refrain,
Whispers of nature, in harmony it stands.

Beneath the pale sun, shadows gently play,
Fields wrapped in silver, an enchanting sight.
As the world awakens, the night drifts away,
Meadow dances softly, bathed in morning light.

Every blade of grass, a story to tell,
In the embrace of calm, time seems to suspend.
Nature in slumber, under frost's gentle spell,
The heartbeat of earth, a melody to mend.

Spring's breath approaches, the warmth will return,
But in these frosted moments, we linger and sigh.

For in the stillness, our spirits can yearn,
Embracing the beauty, as we say goodbye.

The Embrace of Winding Roads

Curves that beckon, whispering secrets untold,
Through canopies of green, where wildflowers roam.
Each bend a promise, of adventures bold,
Where memories linger, and wanderers feel home.

The tireless journey, a tapestry we weave,
With every mile, new stories arise.
Underneath the vast sky, where dreams interleave,

The horizon calls forth, with its shimmering ties.

Through valleys and hills, with each turn we take,

Nature's embrace guides our ever-questing hearts.

Life's winding roads weave the paths we make,
In the dance of the journey, every moment imparts.

So drive on, dear traveler, let your spirit soar,
Amidst laughter and longing, let the wander be free.
For the embrace of the road offers so much more,

In the heart of adventure, we find who we'll be.

Whispers of Falling Leaves

Gold and russet flutter, in a soft ballet,
Whispers of autumn, in the crisp, chilled air.
They twirl like secrets, carried far away,
Speaking to the earth, casting dreams everywhere.

Beneath the ancient trees, the ground wears a crown,
A tapestry woven with nature's best grace.
Each leaf a memoir, of summer's renown,
Fading gently to rest, in this sacred space.

As twilight descends, in hues of deep flame,
The world stands enchanted by this fleeting glow.

Each falling leaf echoes a sorrowful name,
Yet in their descent, we learn to let go.

For beauty resides in each soft, whispered sigh,
From branches to soil, love's cycle persists.
Though seasons may change, as the days slip by,
Whispers of falling leaves linger in mist.

The Golden Hour's Embrace

When the sun dips low, and the world turns gold,

Time pauses briefly, in a magical glow.
Shadows stretch long, as stories unfold,
In the tender embrace of twilight's soft flow.

Fields bathed in amber, kissed by the light,
Moments suspended, where dreams start to gleam.
In the hush of dusk, everything feels right,
As hearts gather close, lost within a dream.

Colors collide in the painting of sky,
Brushstrokes of warmth on the canvas of night.
Underneath this spell, we learn how to fly,
Through the lens of the heart, we navigate light.

So linger in this hour, where moments entwine,
Let the golden embrace wrap you in peace.
For in these sweet seconds, our spirits align,
In the glow of forever, may joy never cease.

Chronicles of the Withering Bloom

In twilight's embrace, the petals decay,
Whispers of time in the softening grey,
Each droplet of dew holds a secret untold,
As stories of summer slowly unfold.

Beneath the weight of the waning sun,
The dance of the flowers has slowly begun,
A symphony played on the strings of the breeze,
In the silence of dusk, a nostalgia that frees.

They tell of the seasons, of laughter and tears,
Of dreams that once glimmered, now dulled by the years,
But even in fading, there's beauty to find,
In the chronicles wrinkled by time's gentle mind.

So cherish the petals before they are gone,
Their fragrance may linger, though daylight has drawn,
In every withering bloom, wisdom finds room,
A tale of existence—a life in full bloom.

The Call of the Swaying Grasses

The grasses are swaying, a gentle ballet,
Calling to the wanderers lost in the fray,
With a rhythm so simple, so pure and so free,
They beckon the hearts yearning to be.

In whispers they share secrets of the land,
The stories of rain and the touch of the sand,
Each blade holds a promise of sun in the skies,
As twilight descends, and the daylight dies.

The breeze carries laughter, a story unspoken,
Of lovers who roamed where passions were woken,
With every soft rustle, a memory stirs,
In the hush of the evening, the heart gently purrs.

So heed the call of the swaying grasses,
For in their embrace, time gently passes,
A reminder of life's constant sway,
Of joy in the journey, come what may.

Murmurs Through the Gnarled Trees

Beneath the expanse of a starlit dream,
The gnarled trees murmur, their shadows in theme,
With roots deep in memories, stories unfold,
Of lovers and legends, of dreams bought and sold.

The wind carries echoes of laughter long past,
And whispers of secrets, too precious to last,
Each branch is a chapter, each leaf an embrace,
In a world where time moves at a delicate pace.

Through the moonlight that dances on bark weathered fine,
The tales intertwine like the branches that twine,
In the stillness, there's wisdom, a knowing we seek,
From the voices of nature, both gentle and meek.

So pause by the trees, let their murmurs be heard,

In the rustle and sway, there's a life in each word,

For in the gnarled branches, the universe cries,
Of the beauty in living, beneath ever-changing skies.

Twilight in the Garden of Memories

In the garden of memories, twilight does gleam,
As shadows stretch long, like a soft velvet dream,

The roses remember the whispers of night,
While the stars peek through vines, shy with delight.

Old paths are woven with laughter and tears,
In the silence of petals, rest the lingering years,
Each bloom is a story, each fragrance a trace,
Of moments that linger in time's tender embrace.

As crickets compose their nocturnal refrain,
The moon spills its silver on soft windowpane,
While the breeze hums a tune of long-forgotten love,
In the garden where echoes and memories rove.

So wander the twilight and cherish the glow,
Of a garden that houses all the joys we know,
For in every whisper, a heart deeply sighs,
In the twilight of memories, true magic lies.

Milton Keynes UK
Ingram Content Group UK Ltd.
UKHW032036191024
449814UK00010B/472